JOURNEY
—into—
PRAYER

Delia Smith

Catholic Truth Society

First published 1986 by the
Incorporated Catholic Truth Society
38-40 Eccleston Square, London SW1V 1PD

Journey into Prayer is based on a series of articles originally appearing in the *Catholic Herald*.

Front Cover: Girl Praying, Gwen John.
Collection of Mr and Mrs D. Little.

ISBN 0 85183 660 7 AC

Printed by Staples Printers Rochester Limited,
Love Lane, Rochester, Kent.

One

IF I WERE to be given just one word with which to communicate the seemingly complicated subject of prayer, the word I would choose is *simplicity*. Simplicity is the key that opens the door of obscurity to let in the clear breeze of God's wisdom and refresh our jaded minds.

It is on just such a refreshing note that the author of the Book of Wisdom opens: 'Seek the Lord in simplicity of heart, since he is to be found by those who do not put him to the test.' There, in a nutshell, is the whole subject of prayer.

If we are seeking God with that pure simplicity of heart, then we are utterly sure of finding him. Wasn't that his great promise to us: 'Those who seek always find' (Luke 11)? As we seek him, so shall we find him in the same measure, and finding him we shall come to know him — not in a vague, notional way but in a deepening, intimate way.

Prayer, then, is a journey into faith, a faith

which grows and develops along the way like (to use the familiar metaphor) the tiny seed hidden in the earth and growing in darkness: though we do not see it, we await its blossoming.

As the measure of our knowing God increases, so does our faith; and as we know him so we learn to trust him. The pinnacle of faith is total trust, and anyone who has scaled this pinnacle has found heaven on earth, because the fruit of total trust is 'the peace that passes all understanding'.

In the office of readings for Lent the Church reminds us of this spiritual journey to which we are all individually called by following the great Exodus story. For that is a journey of faith we can follow today: we are called out of slavery into the wilderness of faith, we learn to confront our enemies and trust in the God who goes before us to the promised land of peace.

In that stubborn band of Hebrews we can see ourselves, often incredulous, too easily content to live with oppression rather than risk the journey. Their journey, like ours, was filled with mistakes and failures and painfully highlighted the limits of human nature.

Yet at the same time, what hope this story holds

out! In it we can see how God deals with our incapacity. When they failed to believe, and failed to trust, he tried again. His relentless love reaches out to draw us into a relationship. Listen how clearly scripture describes his role in that journey: 'In the waste lands [unbelief] he adopts us; in the lowly deserts of the wilderness [our darkness] he protects us, rears us, guards us as the apple of his eye. Like an eagle watching its nest, hovering over its young, he spreads out his wings to hold us and support us' (Deut.32).

The spiritual journey is one in which we learn by experience how to grasp this love with certainty. But we can only arrive at that point if we have the will to make the journey at all. However inadequate we feel, somewhere deep within us we must *want* to make it.

Of course, like the Hebrews, we lack faith — but note: they only learn *on the way*. It is only the experience of the reality of God's promise that fortifies them in faith in spite of repeated failures. When we have seen the Red Sea parted — or something similar — in our own lives, only then can we grasp God's power and learn to trust.

God sent Moses as mediator between him and his

people, but in our age he has come himself. By sharing our pain and frustrations and helplessness, and by knowing what human sorrow is, Jesus teaches us as we are and where we are. His words to one who was about to embark on this journey are words for each of us: 'If you only knew what God is offering, and who it is who asks you . . .!'

Like the Hebrews, and the woman at the well, we cannot know until we start and learn to know who Jesus is and what he is offering. The woman at the well takes the first step by making a decision: 'Give me some water.'

That's our decision too. Do we want to know God? Do we want to receive what he is offering? Will we follow him like the sheep in John 10, who learn to 'know' his voice? Will we allow him to lead us across the desert of our lives?

Jesus's own explanation to his disciples says a great deal to me about the nature of prayer: 'If anyone loves me he will keep my word, and my Father will love him, and we shall come to him and make our home in him.'

If anyone loves me: this is the decision for God. Love is not a way of feeling but a commitment, a two-way commitment, a covenant relationship as it was on Mount Sinai.

And we shall come to him: Prayer is not something achieved by our own effort but something received once we have made the commitment.

And make our home in him: By desiring God, by listening to his word and allowing it to penetrate, I am opening myself to that encounter where my spirit is touched by the spirit of the living God himself—so that I gradually become infused with his own life. It is a process enshrined in that most beautiful of prayers, 'Come Holy Spirit and enkindle in me the fire of your love.' Then each individual life that surrenders to this journey, this process of becoming infused with the life of God, becomes part of his new creation which furthers the renewal of the face of the earth and the coming of his kingdom.

Two

BUT THIS is the *end* of the story. Now let's go back to the beginning. Prayer begins with a decision. True prayer isn't possible unless there comes a moment in our lives when we consciously *choose* to want to know God. Like the woman at the well, we may not know exactly what we want, but somewhere deep within us we turn towards him for the answer.

To understand how this happens I think we first need to reflect on what—in a personal sense—can bring about this decision. Every single human life is a unique and special gift of God's fashioning: he is intimately involved in the fabric of our being, forming and shaping our lives, continuing the work of our creation.

We can know this in truth yet be unable to grasp the mystery: like the psalmist we have to concede 'too wonderful for me is this knowledge'. The awesomeness of this gift, each individual human life, has to be reflected on — and prayer begins with reflection.

Consider the miracle of your own life. No-one who has ever lived has had a face, or a voice, quite like yours; the very imprint of your thumb is a mark of your individuality and complexity.

You are like a rare and precious gem that cannot be matched. Once again the psalmist is intuitively catching the awesomeness of the gift of his own creation when he cries out: 'I thank you, God, that *I am wonderful!*'

The simple truth is that God created you because he wanted *you* exactly as you are, and, as you are, to have a relationship with you.

In this relationship we start out, in Paul's descriptive words, as empty vessels. But that empty vessel, which is me, has unlimited capacity because my life — again in Paul's words — has the capacity (if I enter into that relationship) to be filled with the utter 'fullness of God'.

This is what we need to grasp if we are going to look at the roots of what eventually becomes a decision for God. The empty space will be experienced as a sense of incompleteness, a deep yearning for something we cannot put into words.

It is an experience beyond the level of senses, of hunger or thirst or sexual feelings. It is really that I *want* something but I don't know what it is. It creates an inner tension, a feeling of dissatisfaction that I have described elsewhere as a 'deep-down ache'.

There are ways of anaesthetising that ache: by seeking satisfaction in other things, by creating god-substitutes, 'carved idols' to use the biblical image. There are bigger and lesser idols, work, frantic activity, ambition, material gain, sport, perfection in the house or garden . . . all good things, all God's gifts, but how subtly they can dominate our lives in our attempt to fill the aching void.

Sometimes as we get older, and perhaps achieve our goals, we begin to get an inkling that things don't measure up and satisfy us in the way we thought they would. The ache begins to resurface and again we face our lack of fulfilment. Many people are very vulnerable at this stage. Perhaps they drive themselves harder, or drink more, or take drugs, or have affairs. In her inspiring book *To Believe in Jesus* Ruth Burrows explains it like this: 'What from the outside seems to us sin and wickedness, is not so in God's eyes. Is it any more, I wonder, than the frantic screaming of a child in the frightening darkness of the night?'

For the prodigal son it was necessary for him to plumb the very depths of his darkness before he could make that all-important decision to journey back into relationship with his father.

For many of us the decision won't be so dramatic. It will take a lifetime. But until we breathe our very last breath God will be patiently — relentlessly — 'standing at the door and knocking', awaiting our decision to open up and allow him to fill us with the life he longs to give us.

We cannot attempt to begin the journey of faith and prayer until we *have* made this decision. St Teresa of Avila said it's not with many words that he hears us but in the silence of our longing. It has nothing to do with the outward show of religion, or being a person of high principles and good works. He can 'hear' our longing from the gutter, as he did when the woman washed his feet with her tears.

If we feel inadequate, Jesus himself has a reassuring little story about prayer. 'Two men went into the temple to pray . . .' it begins. The one who was doing all the right things didn't know either himself or God: he was practising religion not faith. The other man was in touch with his own dire needs, 'he hardly dared raise his eyes'. Yet *he* had discovered his own longing: in his wretched state he had come to the temple *to pray*. What hope this story holds out for us. For Jesus said that this was the man who went home at rights with God.

Prayer, then, begins with this all-important decision for God, a decision in which we are prepared to begin reflecting on the meaning of our existence, and get in touch with that inner longing, that 'hunger and thirst' that he alone can satisfy. For he has promised: 'He who comes to me will never be hungry, he who believes in me will never thirst' (John 6).

Three

HAVING MADE the all-important decision to begin to seek a deeper personal relationship with God in prayer, the next stage of our spiritual journey is to ask how, in a practical way, can I seek him and know him?

The answer is deceptively simple. I say deceptively because to grasp it we need to be very simple ourselves.

The whole theme of the Bible is of God constantly reaching out to draw people into relationship. We must try to understand that in some inexplicable way our desire for God is inspired by his own desire for us, and that it is he who is the initiator of the relationship. We can see this relentless pursuit enacted in the history of Israel, and how we can interpret it on a personal level.

The theme of the fourth Eucharistic prayer illuminates this process: God forms us in his own likeness. Even when we disobey him, and lose his friendship he never abandons us but helps us to seek and find him. Again and again he offers us a covenant (relationship); through prophets he teaches us to hope for salvation. The climax of the prayer is God's desire for us (He 'so loved the world that in the fullness of time . . .').

God has actually provided us with the simplest way of knowing who he is—by coming to teach us himself. Through Jesus we have access to all that God wants to teach us about himself. By sharing our poverty, our frail human nature, God has made himself totally accessible, teaching us on a human level how to have a relationship.

Isaiah caught this wonderful vision: '. . . they will be taught by God' (ch.54), the same passage that Jesus quotes, telling us how 'to hear the teaching of the Father, and to learn from it is to come to me'.

To know God, then, we must know and learn from Jesus—it's as simple as that. Like the disciples on the road to Emmaus we can learn to recognise him in the breaking of bread, the Mass, and in the Scriptures. Just as Jesus showed them that everything written in the Bible was about himself (Luke 24) and 'opened their minds to understand the Scriptures', so will he for us if we are truly seeking him. God is initiator and teacher: we are the recipients. As Paul wrote to the Corinthians, 'It's all God's work.'

So what must we do to receive this gift of intimate relationship through prayer? First, we must have the right attitude—which means not setting out to do something for God, but rather allowing him to do something for us.

But then, and most important, we must set aside time, prime time. It is impossible to have a relationship with anyone unless you're prepared to spend real time with them. So it is with God. Reflection is only possible when we have provided ourselves with space.

The enemy of prayer is activity. When Moses came to tell the Hebrews the good news of their redemption from slavery, Pharoah (their adversary) responds with the edict 'increase their work so that they have no time to listen'. The adversary's work has changed little today, and we can so easily become slaves to activity—which is why I emphasise the importance of a decision for

God. It's only when I really want God that I will find time.

'When you pray,' Jesus says, 'go into your private room, and when you have shut the door, pray to your Father.' We can, of course, begin reflecting during the normal spaces of everyday life (train journeys, walking, driving, etc.) but sooner or later we have to set aside real time to be alone in the presence of God, in the simple words of the Psalmist, to 'be still and know God'. Jesus himself revealed time and again how necessary this was to him, by going off by himself to pray.

To start with, prayer is a matter of disciplining our lives, working out our priorities in order to make this precious time. At the beginning we can start with half-an-hour a day, but then our goal should be to work towards an hour given exclusively to God. It takes—according to American psychologists—eighteen months to form a new habit, so we must pray for patience and persevere until it has become a habit and a normal part of our daily lives.

One of the obstacles is very often fear: we fear we're not good enough, our minds are full of our problems and anxieties. But we must summon enough faith to believe that it is precisely here, in the midst of our human struggles, that God comes to us. 'Come to me all you who labour and are heavy-burdened and I will give you rest.' God, we should always remember, is not separated from the world; in the Gospels it is sinners that Jesus keeps company with.

Having found our space we need then to learn not just to read, but to listen to the word of God in scripture, taking a little at a time and allowing it to penetrate (in the Hebrew sense, that means learning to listen with the heart). What is so liberating about this is that you don't have to *do* anything, but allow the word to live, the active word of God do something to you, to touch you, to enlighten the eyes of your mind.

This is where the simplicity we talked of at the beginning comes in. The Pharisee's problem was that he needed to *be* somebody to offer God something; the publican, who went home at rights with God, had empty hands. To pray we need to be simple and receptive, to have the attitude of a little child. St Therese of Lisieux understood this: 'I expect nothing of myself,' she said, 'but everything of God.'

If we are willing to fight to find time for God, and if we're humble enough to listen and allow his word to touch our inmost hearts, then we are truly praying at the deepest level—letting prayer happen, letting God infuse our lives with his own. It is a touch that heals deaf ears and blind eyes, and awakens hearts to the newness of resurrected life that is eternal.

> When our hearts are wintry, grieving or in
>   pain,
> your touch can call back to life again
> fields of our hearts that dead and bare have
>   been,
> love is come again like wheat that springeth
>   green.
>
> (Easter hymn)

Four

'Oh come to the water all you who are thirsty.
Come to me and listen to my words, hear me
and you shall have life' (Isaiah 55:3).

WE started out on these short meditations on
prayer by underlining the need for simplicity,
because it is simplicity that provides us with a short
cut on the spiritual journey. If we reflect on the
words of scripture above (the words that are read
out during the Easter Vigil) and compare them with
Jesus's own words in John 8, 'if you make my
word your home, you will learn the truth and the
truth will make you free,' we have all the
instructions we need to set out on that journey of
faith which is prayer.

Hear! Listen! The words echo through the
scriptures. If we *want* to know God, to receive the

life he longs to give us, we must find the time in our lives to listen: we must learn to listen not just with our ears but with our hearts. God, we have to remember, alone is our spiritual director and guide, and our role is one of receptivity. In the Old Testament conversion (or a decision for God) is likened to circumcision of the heart — as though a hairline crack were being formed in my deepest centre which begins to open me up to receptivity. Then, if I am prepared to find time to listen to the word of God, my capacity to listen with the heart will grow at ever-deepening levels.

In the process of this gradual awakening to the living presence of God in his Word, I will discover the truth of the Book of Revelation: 'If anyone *hears my voice* and opens the door, I will come in and share his meal *side by side.*' The same idea — that the word of God renders our own striving unnecessary — occurs in the Old Testament too. 'No, the word is very near to you' it says in Deuteronomy. 'It is in your mouth and in your heart for your observance.' We don't have to wonder how we are going to climb to heaven, or cross oceans, to find it. St Augustine, in his own awakening, expressed the truth of it like this: 'For behold you were within me and I outside . . . you were with me but I was not with you.'

The disciples on the road to Emmaus did not recognise their side-by-side companion, but they *did* listen to him as he explained the scriptures. When they finally recognised him, then they understood how all the time 'their hearts had burned within them'. Simply by listening to the word, they had been awakened to their desire for God who dwells within. This is the indwelling of the Holy Spirit that Jesus referred to when he said to his disciples: 'You *know* him because he is with you, he is in you.'

Can we be simple enough to believe? We have the witness of others who believed in this simplicity: St Therese of Lisieux desired to go the whole way with God and become a saint, but she also accepted her own human limitations. If it was to happen, then only God could bring it about. Instead of trying to climb the steep slope to the spiritual summit purely by her own efforts, she asked God to provide her with a lift! In other words, if she was going to get there, God would have to carry her there himself!

To summarise the most significant landmarks on the journey of prayer:

First, do we want God? If we do then we will be prepared to seek to know him by providing time and space in our lives to listen to his word in scripture (and in particular the gospels).

As we seek him, so we shall find him (Luke 11), and as we find him so will our faith increase. The work involved in creating this time and space for listening and reflection will be like building a house on a solid rock-like foundation: if we succeed our growth in faith will be able to withstand the traumas of everyday life (the psalmist's 'storms of destruction'), and we will retain a deep peace and serenity whatever the disturbances on the surface.

Finally, as we grow in this intimate relationship with God which we call prayer, and gradually learn to respond to the spirit dwelling within us, so we shall receive the 'life' promised in Isaiah. Jesus reiterates this promise: 'If a man is thirsty [wanting God], let him come to me [relationship through prayer]. Let the man come and drink who believes in me [faith]. From his breast shall flow fountains of living water' (John 7).

In short, whoever makes the commitment to seek God in prayer will receive life, God's life that manifests itself in love. Prayer is ultimately a journey into loving, where first of all we learn to love God (by commitment not by feelings), and as we learn to love him so in turn we learn to receive his love, and to love ourselves. Then we are truly free to love others, not in a forced, 'striving' way but with an instinctive love that is inspired by God's own relentless love for us.

Let's end with one of the most beautiful prayers in scripture, Paul's prayer for the Ephesians, which in its simplicity encapsulates all I have tried to say in these meditations:

May he give you the power through his Spirit for your hidden self to grow strong, so that Christ may live in your hearts through faith, and then, planted in love and built on love, you will with all the saints have strength to grasp the breadth and length, the height and depth, until knowing the love of Christ, which is beyond all knowledge, you are filled with the utter fullness of God.

(Ephesians 3, 16-19.)